what it means
to feel

human

what it means to feel

human

human

trigger warnings for depression, eating disorders, self-harm, emotional abuse, realistic psychological depictions, body shaming, suicide and alcohol abuse.

what it means to feel

for kit, seth and joey

spanning over twenty years
sleeping underneath my bosom
has been my heart beating
has been the pulse spreading
from touch to touches
from atoms to atom

and laid into these pages
articulated with ink
woven with machines
are the words i heard
in the silence of screams
in the songs unwritten

this is the past speaking to your present
this is the book held for your future

this is what it means to feel

human

table of contents

this is what it means to feel

starved

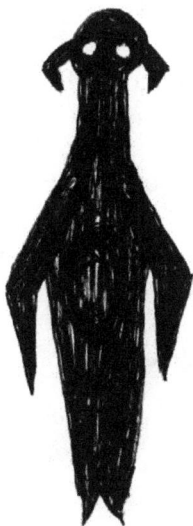

what it means to feel

i have

have you ever held it in
so long
you forgot it was a secret
you forgot no one knew about it

have you ever placed your universe on a scale
hoping
that you'd discover it's worth
that you'd gain some kind of enlightenment

have you ever been so tired
the weight
was so heavy you began to fade away
and so heavy you forgot the last time you slept

have you ever been so dead
and alone
you decided not to shower another week
you decided it's okay that no one knows

have you ever been so desperate
to love
that other's seem so alien
that other's stay far away

human

have you ever wanted to live
so bad
you fucked yourself up to feel the pain
you fucked yourself hard to know you're alive

i have

what it means to feel

haiku i.

he sits quietly
singing happy birthday to
himself but no use

human

wishing

i climbed rooftops so high
just so i could scream
i wish
but what i wish for
is something i never
should have missed

what it means to feel

first foundation

my father is the wall of cracked stone and grime
sinking into the moat we drink

my mother is the old sundial in the courtyard
telling times that no one will read anymore

my siblings are the alleyways to the mountains
tempting homunculi to follow back behind

my dog is the tallest tower in the kingdom
touching the sky where no one can fly

i am the village soothsayer singing alone
traveling through the forest looking for home

a family in a tapestry hung along noble walls
ignored deprecation is taken for decoration

human

roles

bambi became his own mother

what it means to feel

no home

i have eight other siblings
and yet
this house still feels
just as empty
as the day we moved in

human

how will i grow

dandelions don't cry
when they are robbed of sunlight
so i won't either

what it means to feel

runaway

i'm an empty lighter
and a used cigarette
i got a spark
it's there

the sun sets early
my dry eyes burn
but the tears won't leave
there's too much here

there's an old bench at the bus stop
i sit alone with a flickering bulb
i've got no friends
but i'm here

graveyards don't last forever
while i may wish for eternal slumber
the dead aren't asleep
they're not there

i hear the neon signs from my motel room
check the bed for bugs
i shower and the day circles the drain
it stays here too long

human

3:44 AM the pillow is too warm
can't leave with nowhere to go
did i run away from the house or home
i'm not there

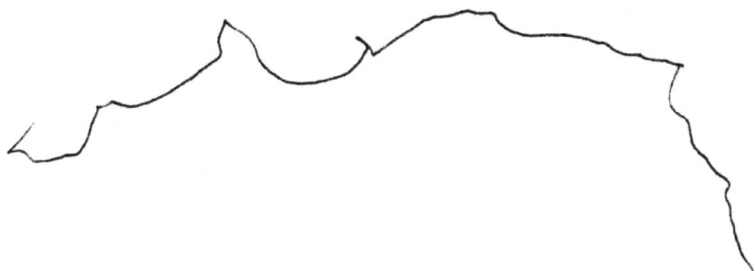

what it means to feel

the path

i'm beginning to dry out
there's wrinkles in my guard
cracking in afternoon heat
under the sun that never sleeps

my feet are sore from cement
but i march onwards for the trail
a path i've never known
the one other's call home

human

quicksand

another step and i sink deeper
into the cracks growing wider

this ground is quaking under
and the jungle grows smaller

uprooting begins logs are sliced
lumber towers are tumbling over

they're rolling into this hole
barking up against my side

as i give in to hugging quicksand
i let my jaw hang and stay wide

let my body feel whole after hollow
for the first time before i die

what it means to feel

fulfill

i'm torn between wanting to live
wanting to die
wanting to give
or wanting what's mine
i don't know what will set me free
but i'm willing to try anything

human

what can you do

if a piece of candy
laced with green
can make me feel like
this

i can't help but wonder
if there's someone
who can make me feel
as good
as this

what it means to feel

conditioning

simon says cross your legs
stare at those thunder thighs
simon says close your eyes
think about past regrets
simon says try to forget
hear your voice beg
for you to change

human

eating disorder

i once watched a show
about a woman who was addicted
to taking laxatives
because she thought
she looked better
skinnier

the next day
i bought the same pill bottle
because i wanted
to look better too

what it means to feel

lies i tell myself

my scaly skin isn't rough
the burn doesn't sting
it doesn't hurt
i'm not hungry
i don't want to live
i don't want to love

human

escape the atrium

the hallways are thumping
heart beats blare behind the wall
shifting the floor hoping i fall
and while i may be on all fours
ending every morning with a crawl
i still vein myself to the piping
circulating around the house
because even if i have nowhere to go
at least i can move around the home
and forget it doesn't get better
when your life and shelter is alone

what it means to feel

naivety

i convinced myself
i'd seen olympus
in mountain lines
and silly obliviousness

like the birdless wind
i flew through airy nothing
let currents carry me
until i finally felt something

human

list

- you told me you and our friends
  had no plans
  two hours later they were posting pictures
  online saying *movie night*
- you told me i wasn't good enough
  by leaving with him
- you told me what we had wasn't love
- you told me after four years
  we weren't best friends
- you told me *it's nothing personal*
- you told me *i hate you*
- you told me *we just grew apart*
- then you told me goodbye

what it means to feel

holding on

here

let me put
all our poison memories
in the back
of the freezer
because i still care
and i still love
and i can't let go

human

oversharing

i give too much
of myself away
but i just i can't help it
when you must share
for others to care
the only hope that can be
is for someone to give back
the same me
i have given them

what it means to feel

teenage wanting

as soon as i was close
i couldn't stand any longer
couldn't feel without her
icy touch chilling my bones

i'm more flawed than most
that i know well and understand
you'll find a better man
~~'cause i'm just a ghost~~
i'll stop trying the best i can

human

wanting (you)

i'm just sitting here
trying to breathe
and i see you
running free
but god knows
i only want you here
with me

what it means to feel

the truth

i want to live

be able to see my life
expand and flourish
become the mountain tops
i dream of reaching
but all i seem to do is want

and want

but i cannot climb anymore
i need helpful arms and legs
to carry me upwards and fast
so i don't wither onto the rocks
and become a fossilized warning sign
though the only limbs i want to help
are my own because i need to be strong for once
i want power but i need it all
how can i want it all when i need nothing to fall

i need to tell the difference
between wants and needs
if i don't i may want to kill me
but i can't

and i wonder why i'm so indecisive

human

just the beginning

you can't fight in battle
if you aren't
at war

what it means to feel

day three

5:36 AM
the sun is waking up
i'm pouring another cup of coffee
each sip burns but not enough

i turn to blue
i don't remember the past few days
my hair keeps falling out
the birds sing and i'm rotting away

with one blink
time shifts at speeds i lag far behind
walking the track with stars and regrets
i put my head down for another soft cry

i feel the cold
wanting to lay on the countertop forever
my blurry vision is a mirage
tears are temporary like the weather

what's different this time
i'm too much for my own company
and flowers take longer to wilt
i'm out of coffee

human

caught

you say
have you been drinking again
though the evidence is all around the room
you want me to lie to you
but it's obvious i've had more than just a few

this is what it means to feel

broken

drinking pt. 1

he chose to live

me

i chose the sweet liquor

what it means to feel

drinking pt. 2

it was on my lips
i can smell poison
on my fingertips
taste so delicious
i wonder why
i'd want anything
but this

drinking pt. 3

if these shots
were bullets
i think i'd finally know
what it's like
to really be
alive

what it means to feel

daily harm

wake up dried blood on my fingertips
something i don't want to witness
anymore

another day of dying with the living
rinse and repeat the feeling deep to my
rotting core

my arms and fingers ache
itchy frequent scratching always shaking
without warning

do i decide the blade or pencil
which do i express first about what really
keeps hurting

human

know defeat

in the mirror stands the undead
still teething never eating the rotting heart

of course this corpse is alive
no one ever seems to think otherwise

maybe the lies i tell are too hidden
under the tongue that never tastes

but i will continue to smile until my jaw aches
until happiness is something i can make

what it means to feel

taking up space

often i think of the end
of what kind of dead
i will become
from more than i am now

if the ghosts from my life
would rather see me burn
into an urn
or see me pressed into earth

after i pass from this world
i wonder if i will live
for the first time
or walk with death again

but i do know that in the end
when i last see the sun
my final words will be
i'm sorry

haiku ii.

the world weighs too much
i want to stop existing
because i'm not happy

what it means to feel

new nature

i.

i love the death inside of me
the violated and the innocent body
dropped off a cliff into a ditch
murdered and fried
that's how i died
let go and behind the future
now i go with nature

ii.

feeling content with the end
the depraved and shrunken brain
forgets how to recall memory
but can still learn how to be somebody
someone new and broken
as i trip down the mountain
with a new foundation

human

nightmare

life is chewing a piece of bubblegum
over and over and over
the memory of flavor keeps the chew alive
after time, time, and time again

the color forgotten and maybe never was
left and left and left you
air fills the gum and pops on cracked lips
after blow, blow, and blow again

a infinity cycle of chewing worsens the jaw
ache and ache and ache
with no taste you add another piece
but never, never, ever will it end

what it means to feel

the problem with overthinking

the more i sat and thought
the more i began to rot

human

lying pt. 1

i'm only happy
when i lie

and i hate
lying

what it means to feel

begging to feel

every time i reach into my chest
my fingers wrap around my heart
and rip it from all the veins
connected to other systems
as i yank it out from under ribs

in my hands it still pumps
oozing vibrating prolonging
as flesh thread dangles over
dripping onto cold feet
and sliding under heels

but the atriums never give in
cut tethers wrap around fingers
sink back into hand capillaries
and sign nerves to send it give back
the heart held now forced into chest

against the will of my thinker
i place the ticker back into place
sew together all the pieces apart
let the beat blare once more
but i dread the ongoing heart

and i wonder why i try
to change what won't die

human

what the sadness feel like

a fog that never goes past my eyes
a siren who only knows how to cry
a mud that never washes off
a breath concealed in a cough
a pitch no one can hit
a wind that makes me slip
a pearl that never spheres
a tooth grinding on tears
a tent lost called home
a walk i walk alone

what it means to feel

drinking pt. 4

4:00 AM
drunk again
my throat is on fire
i feel nothing
but my lips
full of hunger
desire

drinking pt. 5

the sun is up
i'm drunk and i just
wanna have fun

what it means to feel

drinking pt. 6

my tears quench my burning throat
but i know it's not what i want
i just want you wrapped around me
like a warm winter coat

human

haiku iii.

perspective's fickle
can't exactly concentrate
or focus at all

what it means to feel

pulling myself in

i just want to find
my own place
and be alone

human

attempt

this may be the last time

the last time you'll see your friends again

the last time you'll listen to your favorite song

the last time you'll sleep

the last time you'll cry

the last time you'll taste your favorite food

the last time you'll feel again

the last time you'll breathe

under the pills you'll wait
for the breath to leave
too soon too late
close eyes and take the lead

what it means to feel

cotton pieces

even if i sew myself back together
and become whole again
i will always miss
the cotton pieces
i used to have

human

torturing myself

i choose to live the longest
as long as i possibly can
but these needle-point vices of mine
choke my withering throat
they whisper *we won't let go*
we won't let go we won't let go
into both ears
and i contemplate an ultimatum
if i should just give in
or give myself up
to self loathing and impulses i have
but it won't matter since
i don't engage in any form
of compromise because
i won't let go i won't let go
i won't let go

what it means to feel

hometown

i knew this place was cursed
the day i realized
i couldn't see any of the stars in the sky

but now i figure that perhaps
this town and i
might have something in common

nevershine again

i.

my eyes pull towards the sky
canceled rockets of brown iris
long for the shines so nearby
stars laid on heaven's floor
remind me of why i cry
since sleep has left me
i don't dream anymore

ii.

old visions of love have faded
wanderlust walked away from me
out of the blizzard when i waited
in the morning i became snowfall
embodied the winter i always hated
now i travel the world in my head
and walk in my downfall

what it means to feel

at war

my feet ache
my head's awake
dragging my legs across the floor
in a dance of jagged movement
trying to decide who will lead
myself into dead man's land
the dominant
or the dying in me

human

am i getting better

everyday i live in sorrow
and i like to think maybe
things will be different tomorrow
but everything stays the same
no matter how hard i wish it would change

and no matter how i hard try
these tears can't help me when i cry
so i guess i'll just write these feelings out
forgetting how much i want to die

what it means to feel

some kind of dead

it's like
i'm the tombstone
and i want to be
in the coffin

human

by mom

i love you baby
i love your brain
i twisted you
with guilt until
you writhed with pain

i love your cry
i didn't realize
shackling you
to the wall
would make you
want to die

i love your face
i had said
that you're not
good enough
i thought being average
would be
a damn waste

i tried to love you baby
i still do
please know
i was only trying
to be the mother
i thought you needed

what it means to feel

the sun is too bright today

we use a term
like blue
to say we're sad

poets might
say there's a blizzard
in my heart

but this time i feel the heat
my body has become
a blazing desert

i feel off
burns ravage my sight
and body

sweat falls from my eyes
tears run down
the back of my neck

walking the cement this long
usually hurts by now
but i feel fine

am i broken
my senses are mimicking
mood swings

human

i don't know
if i've stopped
or if i'm running in place

squinting down the road
i can't tell if the mirage
is the intersection or me

i feel faint
and this bed of thorns
seems nice

falling back
i peer into the sky
and wait

for the red giant
to swallow me
whole

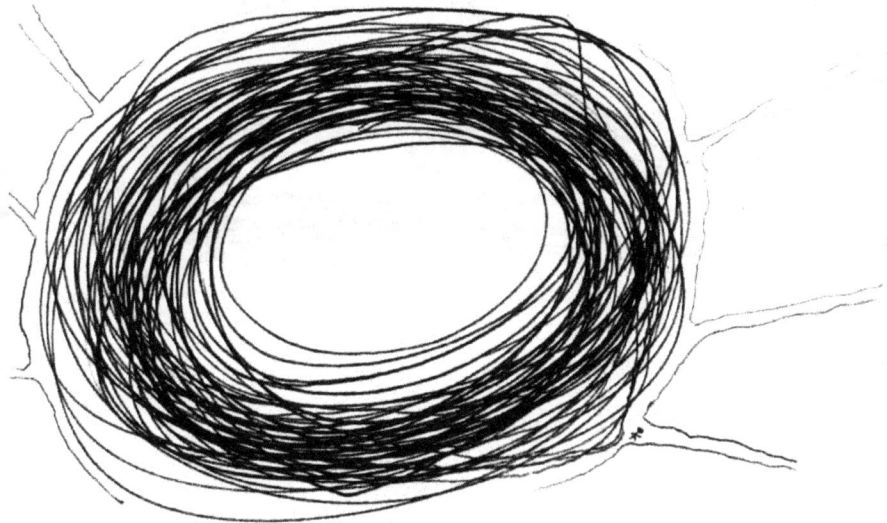

what it means to feel

flashbacks

it's back
again
and again
i keep getting *flashbacks*
about what happened
it's all my fault
about what i did
i'm so sorry
about when it happened before
not again
about promises i broke
it was just an accident
i'm sorry

human

drinking pt. 7

i'm glad i haven't been sober all summer

what it means to feel

drinking pt. 8

there's an excitableness that comes
after a
long
hard
awful
shitty
day
when you know you haven't eaten at all
and you realize the perfect liquid solution

human

pretending as an artist

i wish i was as good
at art
as i think i am in bed

what it means to feel

what am i doing

i'm
asking favors
thinking i'm
the waiter
cause i never seem
to be able to
fall asleep
and i just need
to keep going
but i forget i need to feed
so i glance in the mirror
seeing a few ribs
thinking i look better
even though i'm about to collapse
i still fill my time
every minute to the last
because living
gets harder
than dying
and hoping through dreams
and love
just makes me weep
sometimes i try to leave
escape madness
but i choose stay asleep
this is all i'm used to
all i've known
i don't want to lose that too

human

so in my garden of truth
i plant memories
tagged *something to look back to*
and watch them wilt
'cause i can't hold on
shivering the air is too chill
i wipe my eyes
decide not to get back up
and tell more lies
since all i ever want to do
is sit here
waiting to die

what it means to feel

this happened to me too

you're shirtless and rubbing yourself upon me
but all i feel is the blue corner
and the dry paint i've cried on for years

human

casual sex

the sex
may have been casual
but
it was to blind the reality
that overwhelmed
me

and so
the sex
was something
to cling to
when the walls had no more hooks
i could grab

what it means to feel

it's (not) the same

i just want you happy
but if that means
setting you free
i won't be able to say the same
for me

human

give and take

you're able to put beauty
in everything already full
and i can only place tears
in your glass heart

ocean so clear and wide
inside your inner beater
nothing can crash the waves
that i throw your way

i wanted to be your holder
keeper of the glass healer
you ventured far to find mine
the heart lost from crying

you returned soon after
cradling the glass of another
saying *this one is a little clearer*
now you're someone else's healer

what it means to feel

my strength alone

i was always reaching
for you
but you were never
on the other side

human

what i'm left with

listening to my favorite records
on repeat and i can hear
you

what it means to feel

song material

should i clean my room
or listen to your music
and act like each song
isn't about
how we fell apart

human

i remember

you know
i'm the worst klutz around but
it seems the one thing
i'm good at holding onto
are these memories
that you don't think about anymore

what it means to feel

philip

i forgave the way
you broke me
but i think
you're the reason i don't
know how to love
anymore

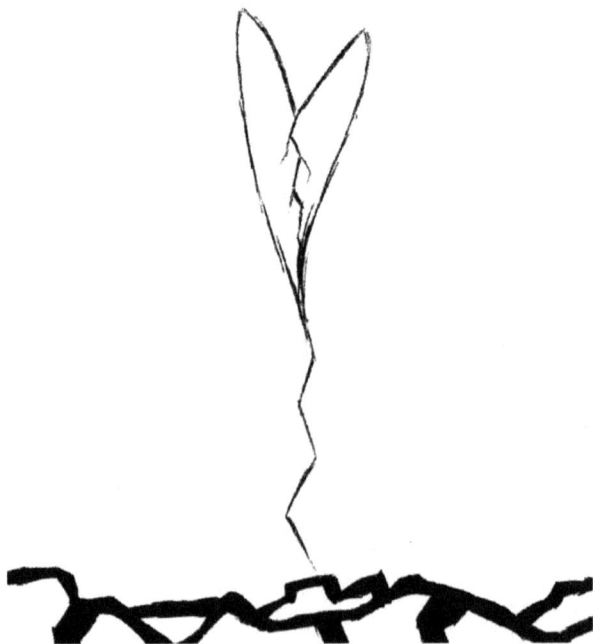

human

you moved on

we washed our secrets down the drain
into the pipes
just so that it can be poured out
into the same cup
you share with him now

what it means to feel

you're not coming back

i left the porch light on
waiting for you to come home
for you to lay in my arms
and press lips onto skin
still scarred from kisses
muscle memory i miss it

i left the front door unlocked
waiting for my love to come home
for you to decorate our space
send vibrations through air
sing in musical mumbles
and say it was all for me

you left me on the porch
and told me to turn the light on
told me *keep the front door unlocked*
so you could slide back in
and keep us sweet as we slept
don't you know i dreamt
you'd never leave

human

this is what it means to feel

loved

what it means to feel

all of you

the beat of your heart
the sound of your steps
the voice in your throat
the guns in your arms
and the sigh of your soul
beg me to commit
to a kind of relationship
i have all but only heard of

human

hooked

you looked at me
when i was shivering
now every time
i think of you
i shiver
hoping i'll catch you
staring once more

what it means to feel

have a bite

i'm ripe and ready to be peeled open
juicy and dripping in the garden
waiting for someone to taste me

ready for the taking of my seeds
this fruit sweet enough to satisfy
waiting for you to come taste me

date night

that night in the parking lot
we were in your car
was warned but went too far
i've given it much thought
boy i like you a lot
our eyes stayed bloodshot

that night was a first
your wanting lips
a quenching kiss
a constant thirst
my heart burst

what it means to feel

break me in

you lost a love but gained a strength
you have an armor that none can pierce
but you don't learn and chose to lock up
you have a habit of lying through your visor
a smile that casts a spell
a freckle that sings beneath your eye
but there's a chip under your shoulder
a itch that just won't scab
you want to heal but you don't want love
you don't want the only way

but you can break me in
you can relax into the sheathe
let the iron fall let the gold show
you can let me use the key
undo the coils in your sleeve
let the breath finally leave
i promise i can take the lead
i promise i won't ever leave

human

haiku iv.

the rose, beautiful
temporal as we are new
but this love is true

what it means to feel

instinct

he loves
and he loves
and he loves me
i wonder if it's a choice
or if it's instinct
and in his nature
to love like him

to hear the sound of his paws
pushing against the carpet
until i feel his warmth on my side
as he nestles his little head in
for a rest it's a blessing
on the one he trusts and loves
for the bipedal one dying
a revival spurs on through the inside
and out as i say *i love you too*

when i finally reboot
i stare into amber eyes
and i tell him thanks for his tribute
but alas it is of no use
i have nothing to give back
no method for making light
no shine for the star onstage tonight
only hands for paws
only breaths for words

human

the wild thrives on inside him
he leaps from my cushion
onto the floor and begins wrestling
with anthropomorphic shells of cotton
until clouds fall out around him
he tuckers out over the rubble
and sighs with blinking eyes watching me
ready to switch and provide comfort

even as he slumps into the carpet
he is aware of the atmosphere
a crinkling snout is always about
sniffing the different aromas
and sneezing at others
but he never pounces on them
he approaches with the same soft tender
used with me

i wonder if there's a way
for us to lay on the same plane
for him to know i see it all
because i have observed
and i have learned
he has given me so much
and now i can give it back
now i know how to *love*

what it means to feel

your body

there are continents unique to you
running my fingers over them
feels like i'm experiencing the world anew
and i am grateful
to be alive

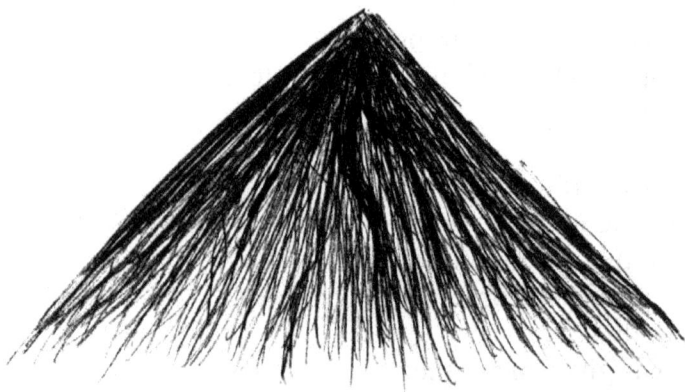

human

passing time

time is you
life fades away

what it means to feel

my favorite thing to do

being with you
is a lot like reading poetry

human

explore me

there's so much
on my body
that you have yet
to see

what it means to feel

infatuated

got butterflies in my stomach
let out by little green men
because i convinced myself
i was lucky
just to be with you

human

help me sleep

i need you
flesh and heat

my blankets can only
be layered upon so much

what it means to feel

geologist's love

you're a rock
in the atypical sense

always still
and ever changing

not afraid of becoming sand
unlike the rest of us

and i think
that's what draws me in

human

a/c

our tectonics are in sync
be both quake at every touch
shudder until the window's shut

our eyes are each other's
just trying to roll back in
every time we kiss forever

we listen to the radio on low
to hear breaths on repeat
only our songs and our beat

we will leave a legacy behind
on the road as we sign in skids
and drive off into the night

what it means to feel

what you do

you fill my canyons with thunder
every time you say my name

rockslides become our kisses
and we let them fall

river rapids flow through
currents knock me away to you

underwater you dive into me
and become all i breathe

human

sometimes i forget

it's hard to remember you're human
when you look like a god

what it means to feel

in the fall

i'm proud our love has grown
into beds and mountains
long enough for me to lay on
soft enough for you to take on

you allow me to cloud the sun
even when i know you love summer
because you know water falls
because you understand my rivers' flow

our garden has begun to flourish
the roses do more than smiles now
i wonder when i will break us
i wonder how many will save us

human

flavor

my skin
made of frosting

yours
made of saline

what it means to feel

making love

you know how to make love
with what's between your legs
while wrapping your arms around me
like a piece of silk string so gentle
you caress the soft parts of my skin
undo the seams of my spine
until you're holding the back of my head
like a babe 'cause you tell me i'm yours

making a fist you grab the nest upon my head
twigs and all
in between your fingers
pulling me towards you i can see lust
on your breath waiting
to fall into mine as we only seem to sleep
in each other's bed
i stare into eyes reminiscent of the night
we first met until i open mine
and realize yours are closed the whole time

rush after rush you flow into me
waves crash into a mountain and i melt
into sand with every kiss and push
you can make sirens cry out
from my mouth in ways
no one else can because i'm

human

your singer
your poet
your artist
your *babe*

we paint this scene the same way every time
using the colors of what i choose to let you do
and what i choose not to say

soon after you've struck the last hour
of what you have to offer me
we'll lay in bed the same way lovers do
in romance movies
because we are in sync and just
so in love

but we don't lie on the same wavelength
you want us to be on

i will fall into slumber
with silly dreams of nigh
unaware you dream a rewind
of you thrusting yourself upon me

i'll wake on the ruins of what our love
should've implemented
see you go on about your day
throwing me glances filled with tones that tell me
i can't wait again for last night
because love only consists of what i do in bed
for you

what it means to feel

i'll stand on the bank of knowledge
with its trickling melancholic rapids
never jumping in time where you'll notice
i don't want you to feel as prisoner
against my tides
if i do you'll realize i'm an earthquake
against a landslide
crushing your little town underneath

i think instead i'll retreat into your arms
like i always do
keeping to myself the terror i could invoke
on your happy face
even if our love is only true to you

human

for better or worse

it doesn't matter
if this feeling is a blessing or a curse
because i'm going love you
for better or worse

what it means to feel

haiku v.

oh my love i'm sorry
i force conversation
but i love though you

human

where did you come from

i cracked open the sun
to find the source
of your radiance

what it means to feel

three names

three simple names
by which you call me
threaten to bruise
in shades of blue

full of rage
the devil creeps
while i lay in bed
next to you

baby

your index drifts across my back
looking for my palms before retracting
to the indent between us

babe

slipping away from sleep
to the carcass deserted in my head
you never saw us die

honey

pouring over me i'm coated in you
wrapped up in sugar, your sweet
the only time you taste me

human

but there is
a simple solution
keep it simple
and say my name

call me as i am
and not as the person
you will me
to be

what it means to feel

eternal devotion

i arrested myself
to a prison
in your likeness

human

imagine

if the sky
and the ocean
switched places

if my heart
and your head
was in the right place

what it means to feel

old roots

do you really want me
to unravel my lies
expose all the vines
under our tree

would you be pleased to know
the dirty seeds still breathe
still lay underneath
each root row

human

just talk to me

how you said
what you didn't say

what it means to feel

somehow

i will find a way to love you

human

i can't give back to you

the monster screeches in the movie background
but neither of us scream in terror. you're breathing
on my neck and i'm holding soft cotton for hands.
your smile wraps around the dark room we sleep
as you persist in asking me if i'm okay. you're one
of the first to ask. to care. and i do but i can't feel.
it. i can feel us skin to skin. i can feel your heart.
beat. beat. beat. faster and faster the longer we lay
in your bed. you ask again. *are you okay?* i'm
fine. *are you sure?* yeah i was just spacing out for
a minute. i was just falling out of your orbit and
into the oort cloud and beyond. but i can still feel
you. i can feel the heat as it leaves your breath. i
can feel the pulse as you try to move closer. and i
do too. but i can't feel it. you kiss me. hard. and i
feel the love pouring out of you glazing our
sunday night. i can feel it. i kiss you back. harder.
and drip some saline and taco flavoring left from
dinner into you. can you feel it? can you feel that i
can't feel it too? i can't give back to you. i can
love you as characters and lovers would. play the
part. fill your heart. and when it breaks apart i'll
put sew it together. but i can't love you as the
monster.

what it means to feel

unsure

do i shove you away
or do i breakaway
or do i leave you again
or do i die again
or do i live alone
or do i enter eternity
or do i not

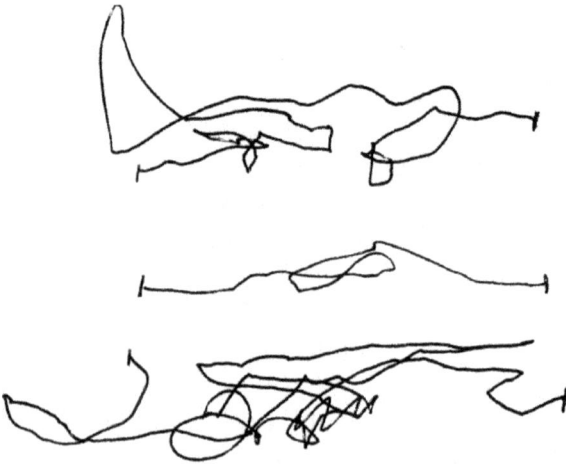

human

stay until i love you

but darling i will try
because my specialty is to overcome
the most harsh of worlds and i will pry
between bleeding dawn washing the cold
and the driest nights you only cry
until you and i can lay under the sun again
without me staring at the sky asking why
i can't find a way to love you

what it means to feel

dreams last

you're hot like the sun
i'm as cool as the moon
under sparkle ceiling
we dance over our tomb

i was your fantasy
you were a perfect reality
grey crowds circle around
we died but were happy

human

this cradle

i've become reclusive
but my passion is present
yours is has always been past
you know this is no way for us to live

starting to believe i'm better
when i stay home alone
because there's no come down
if i wear my own sweater

maybe it's time we let this die
let snow fall over and cover
the house we built together
maybe this time i won't cry

what it means to feel

crime committed

i'm sorry i couldn't stay
like how you wanted me to
i became a recluse
away from your love

i really don't know why
my chest has been hollowed out
but i do know
that i was the one who did it

human

this is what it means to feel

isolated

what it means to feel

trying to be my own

i thought giving into electrics
moving with every second
meant i could pump each atrium
in two separate systems
and be filled with endless love
without an ongoing lover

but i was wrong

human

i could feel you (not)

these little things
these little moments
i dismiss them

you touch me
and i just want to feel closer
you're there
i just want to be close
asking me what's wrong
i just want to feel you
already skin to skin
i just want to feel
for once

i could feel you were here

is this phrase an experience i will ever understand
or hear

what it means to feel

satellite corruption

here let me explain the orbits inside
swirling around the planetary brain
ringing the equator of my inner saturn
crashing water ice over emotional space
falling into my cognitive atmospheres
burning with gravity's growing tug
landing atop gassy storm clouds
lighting it's way down to my center
striking the deep core in repeated bouts
ending the cycle so satellite disruption can begin
again

underneath the crust of your earth you lay
bombarded with craters as i crash into you
loaded with celestial theoretic concepts
corroded as they land with emotional impact
blindsided as my wrecks stir up dust over your sun
bareheaded into the convoluted air you fly
suspended from your undershelter as i let go
reminded of another old lover undercover
impeded by my sincere meteor showers
cemented with my dark matters

human

at the edge of my solar system you came
from beyond the oort cloud in shades
with contrasting hues and blues
i thought my spatial dance was at hand
with andromeda-like features
we could spin into whole oblivion
but i invaded and fell into you
a colossal bleeding dripping over
so i'm leaving to let you recover

what it means to feel

but

did i prick the rose with my thorns

human

haiku vi.

you're underneath my
fingernails; i can't get you
out no matter what

what it means to feel

sex holds me

the epitome
of intercourse
continues to
evade me

or does it

human

addicted to cumming

orgasms are a lot like fireworks
one moment it takes over all your senses
a magic unlike any other

nothing else can't be felt
except for its grand splendor
and damning boom

but once it's over your eyes adjust
and you see things for how they really are
and you wish to forget again
and again
and again
and again

what it means to feel

stop lying

all that pain
bottled up inside
and you expect me
to lie to you
when i know the hurt
that you have inside
kills you
because i have it too

human

i want (you)

yeah
i'm lonesome
and sometimes it hurts
that my love falters
before reaching its potential
because expression can only do so much
when there's no one there beside me

what it means to feel

the decay

does dying happen in slow motion
with miniscule deaths every second
as the wind blows off the pieces

or does it happen all at once
in sudden stifling of muscles
as the heart gives its last pump

i wonder if the dying in me
has already begun

human

used

breathe me in wrong
cough up the mess i am
and leave me behind

what it means to feel

being the comedian

i was happy
things were good but
only because my exterior
was tough and when i was watered down
it washed away the clown

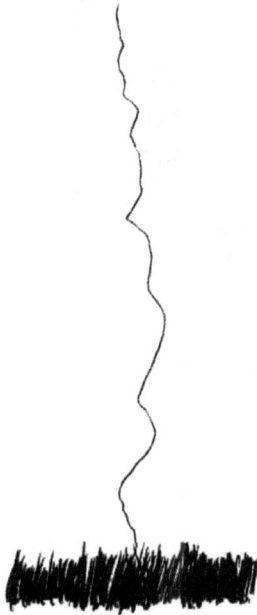

human

for a philosophical love guru

i've been thinking about love
and what it means
heartbreak
joy
or infatuation

why do we crave love
is there a reason
sense of security
sex
or happiness

when someone says *i love you*
is it
loyalty
adoration
or value

what is love
have i ever
felt it

what it means to feel

the high pt. 1

wow

all over
my skin
is prickling
and i
forget

human

not again

suburban streets
of the surreal in my mind
tell me i'm not welcome
and i am lonely
once more

what it means to feel

voices in my head

the quieter i am
the louder i become
my ears are ringing
thoughts are running
screaming
i keep it in but
it lashes out
it's spreading

human

dissociative disorder

my ghost
wants me dead

he places
cuts across my skin
becomes shadows
in the corner of my eyes
and he
doesn't exist

what it means to feel

damned

dragging along the anchor gets tiring
sand stays wet and seaweed never leaves

the rope's in a simple knot but is never undone
i never leave the black beaches my almost homes

but i can't stop the trek along the water
the only place my ghost won't hover

he's there in the distance watching me
following the shells, the steps and path

if i let go the haunting will be my living
and if i keep going the tiring will kill me

human

trauma

yeah
i'm used to the drowning
but each time
the water
forces itself back in
i live again
in my cries
my fears
and
my apathy

what it means to feel

therapy coercion

my therapist once told me

you could be the one
the one to save this family
and bring them all together

i declined the offer
because it wasn't worth it
when i was my own support
alone lifting a crowd
(for all my other selves)

human

what do i do now

yeah
i'm quivering
because my true existence cannot be measured
and i've spent my life looking for a medium
to calculate it

what now

what it means to feel

i finally understand

you remind me
of everyone else
who didn't understand

i say i have galaxies
swirling inside me

i'm sorry
what do you mean

and i cry
at the mundane or extraordinary
because i am learning
to allow myself to feel alive

i've never thought about that

my thinking
isn't a direct path
leading to simple epiphanies
but rather
planets that collide
behind my eyes
and the debris fires
off my tongue

human

but you couldn't understand
and now
i finally understand

what it means to feel

who

a mannequin pretending to be a customer
ordering a heart i can't afford
hearing music played it's a nuisance
curdling against my ear as white noise
i choose to walk away into the unknown night
the dark light i never wanted to explore surrounds
engulfs around me slow like sunlight
but i feel free
even if my mind isn't here with me

human

depressive episode

no one is staring but i am
convincing myself they are
because at least they can see
that right now i'm not me

people in the parking lot walk away
as i run down the sidewalk in tears
hoping that maybe i can push out
the tar lurking inside my streams

as i cross the street cars cruise by
while the drivers and i lock eyes
watching to see if they know
they're looking at a walking accident

i know i cannot escape
the dark waters that find me
but i also know they will recede
and right now i have to keep wading

what it means to feel

lonely

i think
one of the saddest things
in the world
is that
you can't be
your own best friend

human

8:50 AM

desensitization blooms
from underneath my bosom

what it means to feel

different memories

i always see people remembering
searching looking longing
and recounting memories from their past
to remember *life ain't that bad*

i hear them talk about
the films in their head that they lived through
or an embarrassing scene that made a good story
they smile share and laugh
and remember why it was so important to them

when i try to board that train
the station breaks down and dissolves
the rails unscrew while the train choo choos
and wrecks as the scene ends
it's the same every time

they board the train whenever they please
live in the same scene for hours or days
the film keeps rolling as their movie plays
panning over to the seats they talk
about the good times and happy moments
with cheerful cries and laughing eyes
to remember *life ain't that bad*

human

but i never left the platform
i don't know what it's like to rewind
 to play out the good times and happy moments
to talk in cheerful cries and laughing eyes
i don't have anything to remember
no ticket for another

all that i can recall is the hurt
because all that's left in me is
the pain
the anger
the overwhelming numbness
and the lasting sadness that never ceases

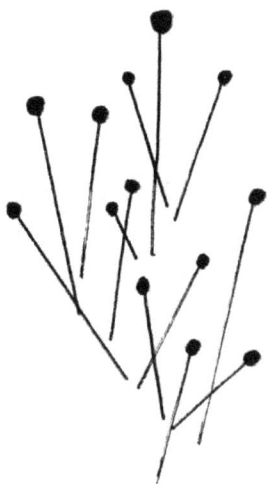

what it means to feel

earthquake

i've fallen
into another fault line
and i don't know
where the aftershock
will take me

human

hormones

sex
is built
into my veins

and i wish
the craving
would end

what it means to feel

what do you want me to do

want me to slip underwater
float down to the ocean floor
and let go of my human form
i already have

want me to make that call
tell of my woes and holes
and ask how to begin filling
i already have

want me to make a scene
burst into wild flames
and ask strangers to drown me
i already have

want me to write a poem
about the terror inside
and the ways i've tried
now i have

human

find me

the coy doppelgänger
left tracks of fragmented memoirs
containing revelations
hoping one day
he'd gain some company
on his uncharted path

what it means to feel

remember this

all the clouds lately
have been migrating
ongoing for a while
just as she intended
as they're meant to
and here i am
the observer
perceiving
realizing
scrutinizing
every little detail
and i don't ever want to forget this moment
i need to remember
that there's other phenomena in the world
so that i won't feel
so alone

human

social veil

sometimes all i see
are streetlights

what it means to feel

in motion

staring outside past the car window
i can hear it
feel it
and i just know
i won't be sleeping tonight
and accompanying that revel
is a house on fire
burning endlessly
placed upon my heart
my judgment
my faith
and only
my love
can save me

human

4:07 AM

i crack open the window
to know there's something else
alive
besides me

what it means to feel

disguise

little do they know
i'm always hiding
behind a wig and
a mask

human

lying pt. 2

how incredible
how remarkable

thanks to all these years
of training as an actor

i can come up with such complex lies
right on the fly without a blink

and i'm able to make fools
of even the wisest people around

what it means to feel

lying pt. 3

droopy eyes
tipping towers of white
lies that pile up
in the corner of my
room are beginning to creep
its way towards my backside
aching with clashing
contradictions i swear i have
no control of

lying pt. 4

promises
sound an awful lot
like lies

what it means to feel

the high pt. 2

i can't be relied upon
when spaceships fly in my veins
and stars explode through my sight

i'm immobilized by euphoria
and the glistening of chimes
i've never heard but can feel

human

the high pt. 3

all i can think about
is the softness of my skin
and the pleasures that induce euphoria
throughout my body

i'm lying in the air
drifting on sky waves
thrusting me up towards space
so i can gain perfect inspiration

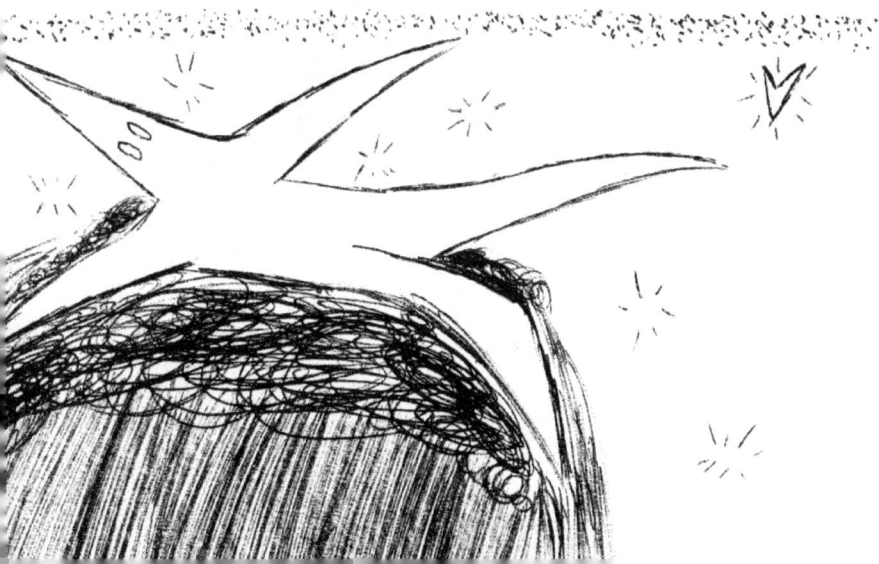

what it means to feel

byproduct

am i the only part of the experiment
that was successful

human

remember the rain

first the mist came. then the downpour. the rain splattered against the earth-strings and played our tune. the only one we were used to. i cycled my sight over the trees until it came back and i saw you. your grin was slight but mesmerizing, as it always was. it's just the way you are and were. but i couldn't stop staring and couldn't stop my heart from beating faster. stronger. maybe it's because it was friday and this was to end the next day. you told me you might never be coming back up the mountain we met on. might never be able to slide our branches underneath each other's again. might need to rip out the roots we grew together. i couldn't let that thought hang any longer. i couldn't let the rotting decay any sooner. so i wrote down this moment for our rhythm to be immortalized. i want to always remember. i want to remember the rain.

what it means to feel

haiku vii.

droplets from the trees
remind me of all the history
we have forgotten

human

make believe i am functioning

sure i got electric spasms
but i swear i'm just like you

twenty minutes of my sleep equates
to your twenty hours so coffee is necessary

these eyes are surfing the plane of existence
but that's just the caffeine

what it means to feel

to alter

a cacophony of sirens
singing songs of every tone
lies within my whirlpool

swirling against infinity
are the tools necessary to build
my own world around me

i wish to honor these blessings
swim out of the deep
and let my heart guide me to the altar

and so it is time to find the shore
finally dig through the sand
until my shell sheds and my heart beats

human

you're gonna lose it

there are things in this world
that we desperately hold onto
but lose over time again and again

yet there's always that one memory
the one that defined e v e r y t h i n g
the one that defined y o u
the one that defined y o u r   w o r l d
the one that defined r i g h t   f r o m   w r o n g
the one that **changed** y o u

but one day

you're gonna lose that too

what it means to feel

this is what it means to feel

alive

human

connect

stand still
listen

feel the wind brush against your ears
you are not alone

don't speak
breathe

grab the earth and feel it's warmth
you are not alone

close your eyes
relax

hear the hummingbirds sing
you are not alone

you are not alone

what it means to feel

new forever

in the heat of the glare
i decide to take the armor off
and let go of the chains

the burns will sizzle
and leave unyielding scars
on moon kissed skin

but within the pain
lies the memory to be
of a time i was me

feeling now free
to walk away from wars
into clear fields

finally lying down
and unafraid of the sun
i fall into deep sleep

dream of the sea
unsand the heart
and let it beat

human

plot twist

you're supposed to save yourself

what it means to feel

fake winging

putting on fake happy everyday
got tiring and was never fulfilling

letting others fake believe in dreams
i never dreamt cost my own faith

wanting to be fake alive to feel
worth living encouraged the bleeding

i'm done with fake living out lies
the truth was never going to die

i see that fake trying won't do
anything but real silent crying

it is time for fake dying to pass away
and let real loving take wing

human

looking back

the depression
could have killed me
but it didn't

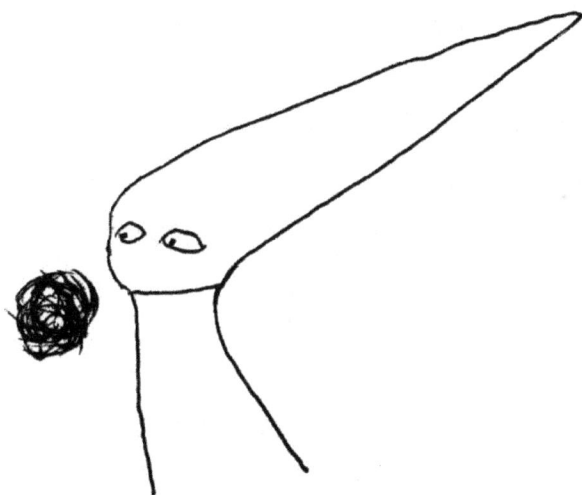

what it means to feel

perception is everything

my life
is accompanied with a rhythm

and the tempo
joyful and exuberant

i feel giddy
as a small child who awes at the world

or like a leaf
anticipating the first drop of rain

and looking around
i notice faces i thought would be like mine

theirs are droopy and unaware
but the zest of life comes from within

their sight is narrow
like a tunnel that shrinks as it grows

because life is what they see
but isn't what it seems to be

human

learning

got off at the wrong bus stop
but i won't wallow in regret

experiencing something new
is to be blessed

what it means to feel

lost in found

i think tonight i will
walk home alone
to old songs again

find myself back in
the drop of vintage tunes
that never left

dance along the sidewalk
cement beats in motion
a swaying vespertine

sweat under moon
phase in and out
the world i see

happy to be found
lost in the evening
with no one but me

human

floating

on my way through the sky
i pass by clouds on the move
swirling over grassy plains
and wonder what it would be like
to be rooted into the ground
forever linked to the earth
always looking up and away
wishing to be the ongoing wind
and wind around the globe
to visit sights seldom seen
by those on foot and sea
never hovering like me
the human close to world's ceiling
drifting in the way of bulb beams
and onward into the sunny heat
letting the burns pass the third degree
as the calm buzz turns to sizzles
i shed off skin layer by layer
and watch my old pieces fall
towards the green from up in silver sky
i begin to unravel and joints undo
ligaments relax and let go
parts among parts slip away
and i undo
relax
let go
and slip away too

what it means to feel

the view

a pinch of the skin or two
for the dream to undo
it's what you always do

tired of the visions that skew
you've been ready for something new
more than just the morning dew

you wander around the city square
stumble and socialize with a chair
discuss your every ware

others never want to play fair
they sit on your shoulder and never care
soon you turn around but no one is there

perhaps it is time to return home
alone where nothing is unknown
but you know the voices will still roam

distant and near they have known
you are their prey shining like chrome
but this is a world only you had sewn

your mind can travel anywhere
now look in the mirror clearer right there
face the fear with a cold stare

human

dig inside through the snakes and snares
watch them leave from your scare
see the gate reopen so you can share

welcome back to the true you
a form from long ago not used to
been underneath soiled glue

feel free and free to feel new
pinch the skin and feel alive too
i hope you enjoy the view

what it means to feel

putting myself first

my vices
and my indulgences

are more important
than you

human

i'm all i need

not being with you
is okay too

what it means to feel

electric avenue

the cogs spin ever faster
steam escapes my mouth
as your words lay into me
slow like falling i-beams
into the nearby antique shops
i used hold closer

the whisper of the streets repeats
in my head it's a mantra
said down my back alleyways
a secret from the rubble
lives on my lips and takes flight
to my ears to be heard once more

i know i'm nothing like you
just a passing avenue to a dead end
but i'm thinking out loud
and i think you are my greatest friend

a sizzle resurfaces threatening with fire
metal walls shudder until they bend
and i give into your phrase
embrace the new hope and begin building
upon stable foundation
for my new electric factory and i say

human

what we have is undeniable
we're both stuck in the eye of the hurricane
but the storm will dissolve
and i will fall into you under the pouring rain

what it means to feel

i've been there too

the bench behind the tree
the tire left on the freeway
the apple core in the trash
the swing at an empty park
the clock with silent ticks
the window never opened
the gold never rushed
the painting never finished

i've been the there too
on the floor
with nothing left
anymore

drifting in and out
of my head
longing for something
never said

but i'm here now
with my feet on the ground
stepping in time
to my own unique beat

feeling the electrics
bounce across the walls inside
i can smile
and say i'm finally mine

human

breathe and walk straight

you can't go through life
doing back flips

thinking that if you don't see cracks
then your floor won't break

because pitfalls are everywhere
waiting to take you by surprise

and if you never confront them
you'll always be the one falling

rather than the one getting up
and trying again

what it means to feel

dj's advice

don't be
afraid to follow
your own rhythm

human

i've been found

i can't stop loving me and it's wonderful

what it means to feel

soon you'll be at ease

if you're like me
and live in a twister
made of barbed wire
tangled up in the misery mire

know that the storm will end
pain will turn to clarity
love will bloom from the deep
soothing the restraints that you keep

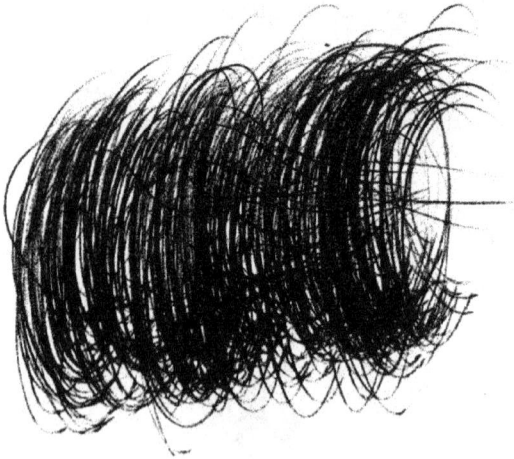

human

wholesome lens

wide-eyed love
is a scope i don't despise
one bit

what it means to feel

how to be an inventor

one day

when the ache of numbing
has become too much to bare
try
    writing
    drawing
    painting
    building
    singing
    dancing
    cooking
    exploring
            something new

let yourself create a world
a wondrous self-imbued atmosphere
through every medium here for you

feel the electrics fire across the body
let lighting scar and wind cut
sleep underwater and breathe in space

the tools to operate are inside
they've been beating as the heart
pumping to know you're alive

human

the inventor has been waiting under
it is time to imagine further
and let magic as love bloom forever

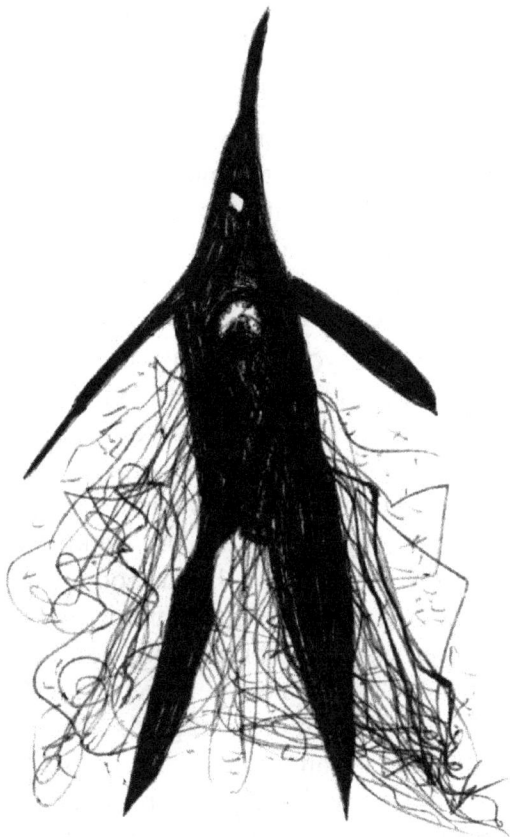

what it means to feel

how to be happy

be honest with yourself. put yourself first. say no
to things you don't want to do. be in touch with
your emotions. allow yourself to feel them
completely. learn not to obsess over them. if
you're sad, be sad. don't deny yourself of things
that are natural to feel. remind yourself that
emotions are fickle. temporary. remember that it's
okay to cry. to weep over the mundane. crying
isn't a sign of weakness; it's a sign of strength and
endurance. take control of your life where you
can. if you're going to school and feel stressed
out, do what's best for you. take a year off. travel.
take pictures. laugh. you can always come back
and pursue a passion you wanted to. tell your
friends how much you love them every chance
you get. forgive yourself. forgive yourself for
things you blame yourself for. we aren't perfect
beings, we make mistakes. it's okay. be kind to
your body. love your body. all your body wants to
do is be your best support system and it loves you
so much. go on walks. observe things you're not
interested in; see from a new perspective. read a
new book. reread an old one. set goals for
yourself. it doesn't matter what they are as long as
you want to complete them. it doesn't matter how
"big" they are. do whatever you can now to
accomplish them. learn. as much as you can.
if your goal is to get out of the bed in the morning,

that's okay too. it's important to acknowledge
these accomplishments because while they may
seem minor, it's still significant because it's
significant to you. and you matter. smile. sing.
sing in the shower, sing with friends. write. write
as much as you can. listen to music. every kind of
music possible. allow yourself to do something
new comfortably. if you feel uncomfortable doing
something, that's okay. you don't have to do that
thing. and love. love, love, love, Love. Love as
much as you possibly can. know that you deserve
to be happy and loved. you're worth more than
anything in the world. let yourself, and the world,
know it.

what it means to feel

you are enough

you do not
have to
be greater
than you are
now

human

a happy life

the king
doesn't mind
being dethroned
because
he's going somewhere
much
greater

what it means to feel

human

acknowledgements

joey. i could not have written this book or let alone have to courage to keep going without your support and love cheering me on. you've inspired me to keep loving. you're with me always.

seth. i'm forever grateful i met you. you've shown me that despite the harsh world that can tear you apart, you're stronger. you've inspired me to keep living. i'll care for you always.

austin. what can i say to such a living star such as yourself? you've taught and helped me with each and every endeavor i take on. you've inspired me to keep being. you beat in my chest always.

third, to my friends and my dog, kobe. i don't know how i've come across such beautiful souls, but you've all told me how proud you are of me. and you've inspired me to keep trying. i promise i always will.

lastly, to anyone that's read this book or any of my poetry. to those who stumbled upon my writings and took a chance on what this poet is trying to say. you've got a piece of my world in your hands and i hope you run with it. i hope the poems in this book will inspire you to be the most true version of yourself.

human

i love you all.

what it means to feel

human is the professional name undertaken by poet, artist, and singer christian campbell, a california native from riverside. preferring he/him or they/them pronouns, human has been creating stories for as long as they can remember. whether it's expressing emotional waterfalls through poetry and occasional playwriting, drawing on blank 3×5 index cards, or composing and singing original songs, they are always exploring their creative limits and pushing them forward. they are enrolled in multiple college courses at riverside city college and are currently studying music. when they aren't completely involved in a creative project, human can be found reading poetry and fiction novels, eating copius amounts of frozen yogurt, as well as spending time with their dog and best friend, kobe. they love art in all forms and mediums, are always willing to explore some new realm of interest, and tweeting about it online. feminist and lover of all things matter and not. @ifeelhuman on instagram and tumblr // @ifeelhuman_ on twitter

human

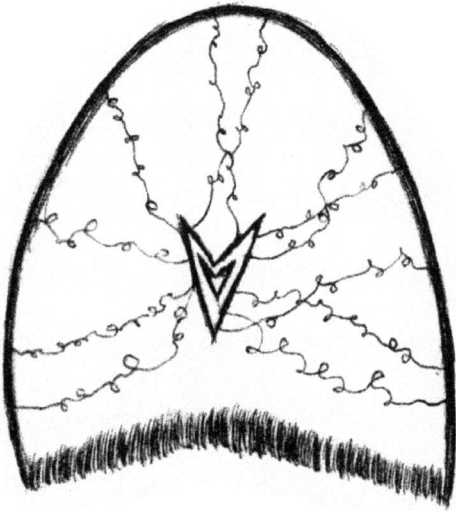

what it means to feel

human